PROVERBS 31 WOMAN

CHELSEA KONG

© 2023 Chelsea Kong

All rights reserved. All images used in this book are licensed copies from their respectful owners including Freepik, Pixabay, Pexels, Unsplash, Canva, etc. This book or any portion thereof may not be reproduced or used in any manner whatsoever without the express written permission of the publisher except for the use of brief quotations in a book review.

Printed in 2023, Made in Toronto, Canada
ISBN: 978-1-990399-38-1
Library and Archives Canada

It is hard to find an excellent wife. She is worth more than rubies. (Proverbs 31:10 ICB)

She is a blessing to her husband and to others.
She likes to make great things with her hands.

She will go far away to get food for her family.
She is awake while it is still dark.

She makes food for her family.
There is always more than enough.

She looks at a field and buys it.
With money she has earned, she plants a vineyard.

She does her work with energy. Her arms are strong.
(Proverbs 31:16–17)

She watches what she does to make sure it is good.
She stays up late at night.

She is a wise woman with many talents.
She has servant girls and feeds them.

She helps the poor and needy.

She is not worried and owns the best materials.

Everyone knows about her husband.
He is makes decisions with the leaders.

She sells the linen clothes that she makes.
She gives belts to the merchants. (Proverbs 31:24)

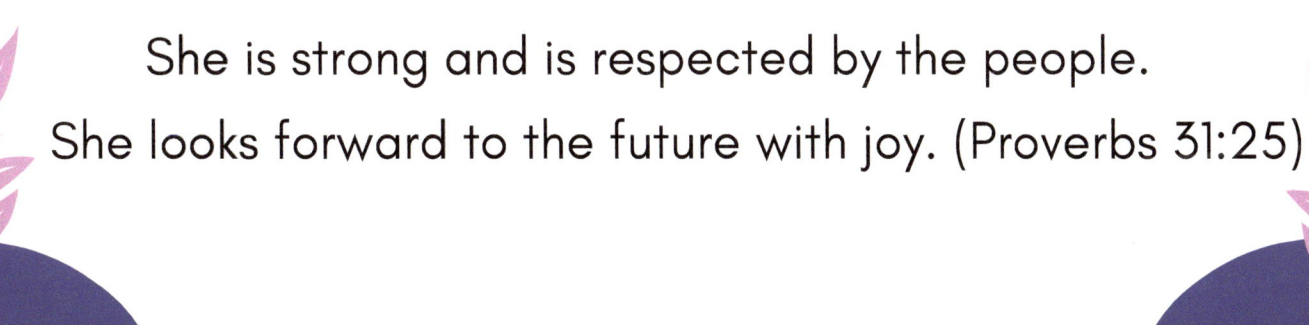

She is strong and is respected by the people.
She looks forward to the future with joy. (Proverbs 31:25)

She speaks wise words.
And she teaches others to be kind. (Proverbs 31:26)

She watches over her family.
She is always busy. (Proverbs 31:27 ICB)

He says, "There are many excellent wives, but you are better than all of them."

Charm can fool you, and beauty can trick you.
But a woman who respects the Lord should be praised.

Give her the reward she has earned.
She should be openly praised for what she has done.

Follow the Proverbs 31 Woman.
Be the best woman you can be for God.

Don't forget everything you do is for God's glory.
Remember Him always and He will always remember you.

He wants somebody who obey Him.
He will give you the best and you more to give away.

He needs somebody who will always pray every day. Read God's Word every day and worships Him daily.

God is the most important in our lives.
He makes all things well for us.

You are special in every way!
Love yourself just as God loves you.

SALVATION PRAYER

God, I know I sinned against you. Forgive me for the wrong that I have done. I believe that Jesus Christ died on the cross for me. That He rose from the grave so that after three days. I can have His long-lasting life. Come into my heart to be my Lord and Savior. I choose to turn away from my sins and I choose to follow you. Lead me to walk with you. Keep me safe and teach me your ways. Stop every bad thing in my life that has an open door to hurt me. Close those doors. Holy Spirit fill me now in Jesus' name. Amen.

BAPTISM IN THE HOLY SPIRIT

Jesus, you are the one that fills me with Your Spirit. Come Holy Spirit and come into my life and fill me to overflow with Your presence. Come with your fire too. Thank you for the gift of tongues in Jesus' name. Amen.

Open your mouth and let the words come out that God gives you. It will be words that you don't know what they mean. You can ask God what it means. You need to let Him talk through you every day to grow this gift.

He will bring you closer to God and you will know Jesus more. You will have power from God to do great things and know things.

PRAYER

Jesus, thank you for the woman in the book of Proverbs. Help me to become a great woman for God and you. I want to become the best for you. Give me wisdom and grow my gifts so I can help others more. Thank you for the talents. Thank you for everything in Jesus name. Amen.

Message from the Author

The Proverbs 31 Woman is loved by many who love the Lord. She is the best woman. We learn from her life how much she can do. She has many gifts and talents. She is wise and careful with her decisions, time, and money. Give your life into His hands and you will see how great your life will become. Give thanks and praise the Lord! Become a great woman for God! Ask God for wisdom and keep using your talents to help others.

OTHER PRODUCTS

- Knowing God
- How to Hear God's Voice
- New Life in Jesus
- Loving Israel
- God's Gifts
- Meeting God
- Word Power
- Fruit of the Spirit
- The Tabernacle
- Bride for Jesus
- A Life of Prayer
- Live Free
- Who am I in Jesus
- Walk in Love
- God's Favor
- Man of God
- Woman of God
- How to Use Money
- God's Wisdom
- Fasting
- See Jerusalem and Bethany
- First Fruit Offering
- Feast of Trumpets
- Day of Atonement
- Feast of Tabernacles
- Counting the Omer
- Festival of Lights
- Glory, Presence, and Holy Spirit
- Live in God's Presence
- Pentecost
- See Galilee, Nazareth, and Tiberias
- Hear God Speak
- Knowing Jesus
- Knowing Holy Spirit
- A Healthy Life and Healthy Life Work Book
- Smokey the Cat
- Passover Unleavened Bread
- Resurrection Life
- The Blessing
- Chelsea's Psalms and Poems
- Revival
- Chelsea Learns Hebrew
- Thanksgiving
- Give Thanks
- Jesus Birth

OTHER PRODUCTS

Coming soon

Loving Jesus: Bride and Groom
Colours in the Bible
Your Daily Meal: Chelsea's Photo Album
ABC's of Faith

Devotionals

31 Day Devotional

Puzzle Books

Biblical Puzzle Book Vol 1-5
Bible Puzzles for Young Children Book 1-3
Biblical Puzzle for Children Books 1-5

Teaching Series

How to Hear God's Voice Teaching Guide & Audio Book
Relationship with God, Jesus, Holy Spirit Guide
Knowing God, Jesus, Holy Spirit Guide & Audio Book
Flowing in the Prophetic

Teaching (Non-Sale on my website)
Purim
Passover
Resurrection

More books to come!

BOOK REVIEWS

More books on Amazon, Kobo, and Barnes and Noble, Smashwords
https://chelseak532002550.wordpress.com/

> More books on Amazon, Kobo, and Barnes and Noble, Smashwords
> https://www.amazon.com/author/chelseakong
>
> Please leave a review and share with friends to help the author continue to write more books to reach more readers. Thank you so much for your support.

Review!

About
CHELSEA KONG

She is a writer, creative arts and digital media artist, skilled administration professional, and podcaster. Chelsea also served in a variety of roles, from audiovisual, photography, to assisting on the worship team, and ministry team. She also has a passion for families being united.

Chelsea has been a guest on Unity Live Radio, The Lady Tracey Show, and How to Live for Christ and is highly recommended by a Proud Christian blog. She is also a guest blogger. A few of her books have been featured in YourAuthorHub, etc. She graduated from Hotel and Restaurant Management, Digital Media Arts, Office Administration, Payroll Professional, and experience working with children. Chelsea lives in Toronto, Canada. She mainly writes children's books, stories, bridal writing, poems, lyrics for songs, words of encouragement, blessings, prayers, and jokes. The author of How to Hear the Voice of God, the Bridal Collection, Knowing God, etc. She also has her own Bible Puzzle books and other inspired products. Her podcast channel is called Chelsea K on Anchor, Spotify, and iTunes.

Please check my website to find out more:
https://chelseak532002550.wordpress.com/

www.ingramcontent.com/pod-product-compliance
Lightning Source LLC
Chambersburg PA
CBHW041414010526
44107CB00016B/1169